COMPOUND YIELD

COMPOUND YIELD
The Investors Edge in a Traders World

ROBERT K. NAGUSZEWSKI MD

authorHOUSE®

AuthorHouse™
1663 Liberty Drive
Bloomington, IN 47403
www.authorhouse.com
Phone: 1-800-839-8640

© 2012 by Robert K. Naguszewski MD. All rights reserved.

No part of this book may be reproduced, stored in a retrieval system, or transmitted by any means without the written permission of the author.

Published by AuthorHouse   08/08/2016

ISBN: 978-1-4772-9459-8 (sc)
ISBN: 978-1-4772-9460-4 (hc)
ISBN: 978-1-4772-9461-1 (e)

Library of Congress Control Number: 2012922393

Print information available on the last page.

Any people depicted in stock imagery provided by Thinkstock are models, and such images are being used for illustrative purposes only.
Certain stock imagery © Thinkstock.

This book is printed on acid-free paper.

Because of the dynamic nature of the Internet, any web addresses or links contained in this book may have changed since publication and may no longer be valid. The views expressed in this work are solely those of the author and do not necessarily reflect the views of the publisher, and the publisher hereby disclaims any responsibility for them.

Contents

Thanks and Gratitude vii

You're at the Threshold ix

Truths xiii

Compound Yield 1

Seeing, Believing, Receiving: Results and Implications 15

Back-Test of Compound Yield on SPY 21

Growing with the Plan and Some Lessons Learned 25

Bottom Line: A Little Rehash from a Different Perspective 53

Volatility Discussion: Some Surprises 57

Maintaining Highway Speed 61

Some Interesting Things 69

Driving This Home 73

Odds, Ends, and Disclaimers 81

The Catalyst 83

Calculation Template 87

Resources 89

Thanks and Gratitude

- To my wife, Tanya. You've always stood with me even through my darkest times. You anchor me and are the source of all sensibility.
- To my daughter Anna. Because you are so much like me, you help smooth out my rough edges and teach me to take each day less seriously.
- To my daughter Sophie. You are my "glass is half full" girl and remind me that God's world is replete with possibility.
- To Henry, Sadie, and Abu (yes, our dogs). They help me understand that spending some time in the present moment is worthwhile. The present moment is where happiness and joy live. I'm learning to let my thoughts gallop less into the future.
- To the instructors and my coach at Online Trading Academy, Atlanta, Georgia. Your information combined with a sincere desire for the students to succeed catapulted me to design the Compound Yield strategy. You've opened my eyes to see that

things are not what they appear. And yes, I finally have written my trading plan, and this is it!
- To John, Jeff, and Julie, my investment team at Scott and Stringfellow, Atlanta, Georgia. Your research, advice, guidance, and patience are appreciated! You've kept your promise to personalize my portfolio.
- To my patients. You taught me that any one life is no less valuable than another and that a life of service is a good one.
- To God and His wonderful universe, where we get to co-create our lives alongside Him.

You're at the Threshold

Now that you have opened the door, come on in! What you hold in your hands is hope: hope for your future, hope for your family, and hope for your community as you will be able to be more generous to it. Just by picking up this book, you have shown you are looking for answers. I suspect you fear the truth about what retirement may look like for you. This book came as a consequence of my own interest in improving my future. The success I'm having has ignited a spark of passion in my soul. The funny thing is that when your soul ignites, the rest of you tends to catch fire as well. I'm on fire with enthusiasm and hope. Because this emanates from the level of the soul, I'm compelled to share it with you. A divine truth of the universe is that to receive what it is we want or need, we have to give precisely that away. To be loved, we must love. To have a friend, we must be one. To have generosity shown to us, we must be generous. For me to be wealthy and financially secure, I must help you get there as well. In serving you, I serve myself. What could be better?

Every book has a little bit of self-centeredness, and such is the case with this one. In a sense, I'm tooting my own horn—but mainly just to myself. At age fifty, over a short period, I lost nearly every material thing I had and was left with little more than my retirement account. For three subsequent years, I lived numb with fear and hopelessness that retirement would not be possible at a reasonable age. The prior ten years in the market had produced no growth in my account. I yearned for a second chance, a chance for redemption. Writing this book has placed a dream again in my heart and the plan to bring it to life. These pages contain that plan, and I will share its formula with you. In reading it, certain thoughts may come to you: *So simple! So obvious! Why did it take me so long to see it?* You will have been blessed. This will return to me, somehow or some way, and I too will be blessed again. I want you to take joy in bringing these pages to life. This is a game-changer for me, and it will be for you.

My highest hope and most grandiose wish for this book is for it to become a manual to achieve the common good. Out of concern for our country and particularly the private sector, this formula was born. For a country of over 300 million, only 100 million likely pay taxes. Conservatively, it would be true to say that the top 40 to 50 million pay the vast majority of the federal tax burden. A great wrong needs to be righted. We are on the road to an uninspired existence as our country moves toward an entitlement society. If you are one of the 50 million, this book is for you. It's for everyone else like us—the private sector. The burdens of the world have always been ours to bear, and we've been well-equipped to handle them by our entrepreneurship, dedication to long hours, and willingness to assume risk. We were generally rewarded. However, entitlement and lack of free spirit will bite off the hand that feeds it. Our country may be nearly there.

This book is dedicated to men and women of the private sector who have worked hard to get ahead; have paid more than their share of taxes; have contributed consistently to a 401K for pitiful returns; and are fearful they may not be able to retire. I empathize. You have taken all the risk to better yourselves, advance in your careers, and contribute to your communities, only to find yourselves falling short of your public counterparts who are protected by defined-benefit pension plans. It is a sad irony that those who pay for these benefits are left with no protection themselves. Again, we need an equalizer, a game-changer, and this is it!

This book is meant to profit you, and to the extent it does, we'll be better able to afford our entitlement country. If the strategy here is adopted by enough people (and I do hope millions will do so), the markets will stabilize. The market sharks, the market gamers, and the dishonest among us will have hard work ahead. When they try to game the market up, we'll be selling. When they short-sell, we'll be buying. We're putting the brakes on unrestrained and undeserved profit. We can become a colossal gyroscope on this out-of-control missile we call the markets. I can only hope, then, that we can return to more traditional concepts of buying great companies at good prices and reinvesting dividends to attain long-term growth and income. Perhaps then, all those who have taken themselves out of the game and are sitting on the sidelines (with trillions of dollars) can begin to test the water again.

The Compound Yield formula is the investor's edge in a trader's market. It was developed to fix my own financial outlook. Its remarkable power in my rollover IRA is what prompted the completion of this treatise. I am excited. I now have peace and confidence that I will have a seat at the table of plenty when I retire. You can join me!

> *"Truly I say to you, whoever says to this mountain, 'Be taken up and cast into the sea,' and does not doubt in his heart, but believes that what he says is going to happen, it will be granted him. Therefore I say to you, all things for which you pray and ask, believe that you have received them, and they will be granted you."*
>
> —Mark 11:23-24, NASB

Truths

As a physician, I am necessarily a student of human nature. Below are truths I hold to be absolute. If you disagree with some of them, close this book and return it for your money back. The entire strategy of Compound Yield is predicated on them and counts on them to be true.

- Successful trading is the movement of money out of the account of an amateur and into the account of a professional. The "lost decade" (past ten-plus years) really wasn't lost at all. You and I saw no progress because the traders' accounts swelled at our expense.
- Buy-and-hold investing has no likelihood of reasonable success.
- It's a trader's market and will continue to be. The accelerated rate at which information can be known will see to that.

- Fear and greed drive the markets. They are friends of the professional.
- Those who do not understand broadly the difference between how the markets actually work and how they are supposed to work will continue to get slaughtered. The best thing I did for myself was to learn about trading by being trained professionally. The investment world is not what it seems.
- Trading is emotional, and professionals count on that when they go long on or short a position. The market-makers, speculators, and large institutional traders will create emotion if there is not enough in the market. Emotion is reactive, and when investors react they are teed up for slaughter. Momentum up is greed—everybody jumping in before being left behind. Momentum down is fear—everybody trying to get out before it's too late. Even if an investor was not reactive and instead chose to sit tight, he or she was left with just dividends. They may be puny.
- A new strategy is needed.
- The obvious is often hard to see, simplicity is better than convolution, and consistency beats gambling.
- This truth I hold unshakable. If it does not resonate in your soul, you'll likely miss the perfection in the secret these pages contain. The universe is consequent to the divine. I have no trouble in calling this God who is the source of all perfection. Any truth discoverable in God's universe shares this perfection. All of mankind has a God-given birthright to benefit from any such discovery. It becomes the responsibility,

then, of the discoverer to share it—hence, this book. I only need 40 to 50 million of you to see this strategy clearly, and we can save our country. I have little doubt that you will self-select yourselves. It is your nature to do so. You and I together will shoulder this burden, challenge, and gift.

This book does assume some knowledge and personal experience with investing and trading for the reader to benefit from the discussion. Emotion needs to be divorced from our decisions so we may be open to the simple and rational. The Compound Yield formula is our edge to win in the traders' arena. It is predominantly defensive (strong risk-management), but any punch thrown (trades) counts.

> *"'For I know the plans I have for you,' declares the Lord, 'plans to prosper you and not to harm you, plans to give you hope and a future.'*
> (The New International Version, Jeremiah 29:11)

Compound Yield

Compound Yield is the term I adapted to crystallize what we are trying to accomplish by this strategy. Effective use of this strategy is straightforward, clear, and truly simple. Even so, it is not appropriate for everyone. It is specifically designed for those who have lost money in the market, have had real skin in the game, and have lost confidence in mutual funds and fund managers. It is for people who have always charted their own course, have gotten kicked in the gut, and have gotten back up again. It is for us, because I am one of those people. For those who expect to be taken care of by the government, unions, or any entity that promises unfair and unreasonable benefits coming off someone else's back, this is *not* for you. You've not earned the right to be at this table.

Compound Yield, operationally, is a strategy that combines high-yield investing with safe trading to progressively produce increasing income. It is an active strategy that, once clear in the user's mind, can be adjusted to suit individual needs. It is flexible and can be used exclusively or collaboratively with other strategies. For me, the strategy evolved out of my need to secure a retirement that a traditional 401K could not likely produce. This book is a complete description of what I've been able to do in collaboration with my present brokerage firm for my rollover 401K IRA.

Fundamental assumptions of a Compound Yield investor that must be understood:

- We are income investors who focus on yield. Yield is the priority.
- Stock fundamentals are significant to secure confident payment of dividends and much less important in predicting price movement.
- Price movement depends much more on trading/being gamed.
- Yield investing takes advantage of "loans" to companies/stocks in which neither the principal nor the interest return is fixed. This leads to incredible possibilities as an investor. Because we focus on the relationship between the two, mental paradigm shifting allows maximum return.
- The only thing *real* is income/dividends paid or capital gain actualized. Changes in dividend payments occur much more slowly than share-price movement. This allows capture of profits in volatility without sacrificing income for profits.
- Allows/provides a plan to enhance yield (income per share price) continually.
- Supercharged process leads to compound yield.

Basic Concept Structure Outline

I hope that what I'm about to discuss will start to change how you look at investing in today's markets. By bringing key elements to attention, we can begin to see how a buy and hold strategy can be optimized to increase income and capitalize on capital gain.

- Find high-yield stocks, preferably with yields greater than 5 percent. Various sources are available. My preferred resources are listed at the end of this book.
- Determine that fundamentals are strong enough to pay the dividend and hopefully increase it over time. These are standard parameters easily available on trading sites. I use a simple E*TRADE account.
- Enter position based on yield and not where the stock price may be in its trading range.
- Trading behavior depends solely on trying to increase yield on the shares held. When shares increase in value, sell enough of that stock to capture profits. The whole position is not sold. By doing this, yield is preserved on the remaining shares held. If the share price drops, yield is increased by buying down into that stock. This dollar cost averages share prices and pushes up yield.
- Size the position. For a million-dollar portfolio, I've chosen $25,000. Where share prices climb, sell enough shares to stay around $25,000. I've chosen this because this was my circumstance. After twenty-three years of sacrifice to save $30,000 to $40,000 annually, my return/growth was a paltry 1 to 2 percent. When share prices go up, sell to stay

around $25,000. When they go down, buy to pull back up to $25,000. The $25,000 position amounts to 2.5 percent of the portfolio and is what should be used to guide smaller or larger portfolios.

- Therefore, buy only into declining prices and sell into rising prices. Never (or almost) buy into rising share prices for any given stock. Buying into rising prices reduces yield. We are yield investors. It is important to remember that income/yield is investing. It is the only thing real. Capital gain/capital loss is *trading*, not investing. We are income investors first and foremost, and we are special ones at that, because we are Compound Yield investors. Buying into rising stock prices essentially is resetting the position to a lower yield. This is the opposite of being a yield compounder.
- Capital gain is money on the table not being used. It looks good on paper, but it's not doing any work for us. Capital gain can only work for us if we sell it to make income. We use capital gain/profits to buy down into declining price positions to increase yield on that holding. We are supercharging our portfolio by taking profits off the table and putting them to work for us. Capital gain left too long on the table will be taken by traders. On a day-to-day basis, stock prices rise and fall on trading and not fundamentals. Again, fundamentals are to secure that the dividend continues to be paid. We decided what yield we were satisfied with when we entered the position. If the stock price goes up, this is gravy. Sell the profit and put it to work elsewhere. By adhering to these rules, we always preserve or increase yield.

- Buying into rising prices is counterproductive because doing so resets the position to a lower yield. Think twice. Be sure you really want to do that.
- The magic is that we compound our yield by taking profits (free-trade money) to buy more shares of a declined position. The odds should be high that our declined stock continues to pay and hopefully increases its dividend because we bought stocks that met our fundamental criteria.
- We can also use free trades to open new positions in different sectors to broaden our portfolio—diversify. Again, we are interested in buying high-yield stocks with very good fundamentals.
- Trading—again, we are investors. Compound yield is, however, our edge in a trader's market, and we never lose on a trade. We know the outcome before we take a trade, that is, capital gain/profit. We take the proceeds from our trades to invest, adhering to the plan. Eventually, great fundamentals get noticed by the market and share prices rise consequently. This gives us the opportunity to do our kind of trading again and again.

We concentrate on high-yield stocks and build yield. Our money isn't sitting around doing nothing. It's earning interest and dividends. We're making a decent return even while little or nothing may be happening to the stock price of any given holding. A growth stock can't do this for us. I consider a low-dividend or no-dividend stock a growth stock. These are the stocks traded for the hope of capital gain. These stocks do not meet investment criteria here.

For a trade to occur, there must be a buyer and a seller. The market-maker puts these two together for a profit. Therefore, *all* trading is honestly or dishonestly gamed by the market-makers and institutional investors. That's why they say "the trend is your friend" and "trade with the sharks, not against them." The problem is that you have to know where the sharks are and how they are going to trade (big risk variable). It's often not good enough to know how the sharks are trading now; you really need to know the direction they are *going* to trade. High anxiety, I'd say, for the individual trader. Compound Yield investors don't have these headaches. We wait for the sharks to come to us, and while we wait, we are rewarded by great dividends and income. When the sharks do show up, we give them what they want. We sell them our shares, but only for a profit. We've baited them by having a broad range of stocks they may be hungry for. Either way, the strategy tells us what to do. If they game share prices up, we keep selling into them until they are tired of buying. We then buy down into our holding should another shark game down prices by shorting them. On the one side we take profits, on the other we increase our yield. What could be better? Either way, we are generating money to compound yield with.

The Compound Yield investor has answers to the difficulties of trading consistently well (tough for even professional traders).

Q: How do we know what the sharks are hungry for?
A: We don't, but we don't have to either. Sharks can be finicky and emotional. We let them decide what they want by having a variety of stocks from different parts of the

market. Diversification, plain and simple. We provide a nice department store to shop in.

Q: What if a stock gets no interest from the sharks?
A: That's why we own high-yield stocks, so that our money is always working for us.

Q: What if the sharks don't like one of our stocks?
A: We buy down into it, increasing our yield. Eventually, sharks will game it again, and we'll sell into them. We've also protected the portfolio by sizing positions.

We always sell into sharks to give them what they want (some of our shares). We want to be helpful and generous to the sharks. They are kind enough to tell us where they are and what they want. Because we know this, we always win on our trades. Beautiful symbiotic relationship, isn't it?

The potential of being a Compound Yield investor is best seen in a self-directed rollover IRA. This is because:

- The fund is closed to additional outside contributions.
- It now needs a way to generate revenue that can be reinvested. This essentially becomes the source of new money, replacing the regular contributions made during employment.
- Because it is a closed system, the results of the strategy are much clearer to see. The portfolio lives and dies by the actions of its owner.

- Because my retirement money wound up in a somewhat self-directed rollover IRA, I was able to see what we've talked about and fully develop the Compound Yield investor strategy from conceptualization to actualization, and it's powerful!

Mechanics

What follows next are the individual thought processes that go into preparing for a trade day. Each is worth considering singularly and then together as a whole. This synthesis produces the conviction to pursue a trade day.

1. *Choose your stocks.* Look for great yield and great fundamentals. My ideal stock has a price-to-book value of less than or equal to one; high return on equity for its industry; reasonably good payout ratio depending on industry average; current and quick ratios greater than one; and good to excellent profitability measures. If quick and current ratios fall short and debt burden is a little high, I may still buy if all profitability measures are at the highest percentiles for the industry. Everybody weights parameters differently. The point is that we want to be confident that in any market cycle, our stock will meet its dividend and likely increase it. It's a great bonus to find a stock that meets requirements and has consistently raised dividends. Just another nice way dividend stocks help us compound.

2. *Size each position.* I like $25,000. For a million-dollar portfolio, this would be forty positions, or 2.5 percent of the portfolio for each position.
3. *Understand trading expenses.* My broker is Scott and Stringfellow. At the million-dollar level, I have personal brokerage, and the management fee is 1 to 1.5 percent on the portfolio annually. The expense fees are collected quarterly. There is no restriction on how many times I can trade. You could, of course, just use an online broker, which would be less expensive, but you won't have any broker advice or input.
4. *Keep your account Web page as simple as possible.* When a position has declined in value compared to your cost, the amount should show up in red. If you are up in a position, that amount should be in green. The importance of red and green is so just by looking at your Web page, you quickly know what stocks you may want to sell shares on and which ones you may want to buy down into.
5. *Take profits at the right time.* For each position, I keep rough track of my current yield on cost/NAV. This is mainly to tell me when to take profits. As an example, if my dividend yield is 6 percent on a particular stock, I probably won't take profit until the share price is up that far on my cost/NAV. I try to take profits every time that happens. Why? Well, if I'm up 6 percent, I've made the same amount of cash in one trade that my dividend would take a year to make. It would be senseless to not sell enough shares to take that profit off the table and use it elsewhere. Kind of "one in the hand is

worth two in the bush." If you are down an amount equal to your annual dividend on a position, recheck fundamentals. If there is no change and no obvious bad news about the company of significance, buy down into to increase yield.

6. *Know how much to buy and sell.* This is exact and straightforward. If you are up, sell shares to fully capture the profit. If you are down in a position, take that amount and divide by the present cost of a share to tell you how many shares you need to buy. Again, by buying and selling, we're just trying to keep our position steady around $25,000.

7. *Go with your instincts.* If shares prices keep dropping on a position and you still feel confident in the stock after researching it well, buy into it. This can be a nerve-wracking, and some investors might want to set a mental stop-loss at 20 to 30 percent of their cost basis on that stock. If it hits the stop limit, then you sell the entire position at market. If share prices keep going up, then you are truly blessed. Keep taking profits until you run out of shares. Talk about a home run!

8. *Have cash available.* I try to keep enough cash on hand in my cash account to always be able to buy at least one new position so as not to miss a great opportunity. Certainly what is a great opportunity for you may be different than for someone else. You decide whether to buy based on what yield you want to start out with. This is not the same as a "good price."

9. *Stay proactive.* Market timing is really reduced as an issue using this strategy. It has always been drilled into our heads

to buy low and to sell high. Yet the market may play out unpredictably. The "market"' is the sum total of its parts, and these are emotional, not rational. There are individual investors trying to buy fundamentals for capital gain. There are institutional investors that move large sums of money that affect share prices quickly. There are the market-makers pressuring prices for their own gain. People short the market, and others trade options. The list goes on and on. The sum total of all of this activity shows up as the spot price of a stock for a moment or two. Eventually, the share price actually reflects its value but probably just for a moment, and then the price changes. What I'm saying is that what the market says the value of a stock is and what you think it may be worth is opinion on both sides. This difference drives trading and not absolute value. "Buy and hold" investors think they are buying absolute value, and they are not. They will continue to get spanked in the market. Trading is emotion being dissipated. We want to be on the upside of this emotion using our strategy to importantly manage longer-term risk. Here is a perfect example. You look at a stock that has a great dividend, but you are afraid to buy it because it is near a fifty-two-week high. Our strategy would encourage you to take that trade. Why? If a stock is at its fifty-two-week high, you're afraid that the price is going to drop. If you did buy it at the starting yield that was acceptable to you and it went down, you would buy down into it and increase your yield. If it goes the other way and had more momentum, well, wouldn't you be lucky! You would keep taking profit until it reversed. Then you would buy down into it. That's a *great* trade! It would be great if that happened every time. You always have the heads-up which way things are going. If it's green, you sell. If it's red you buy. This is a simple rule, to consistently buy low and sell high over and over. The system tells you what to do. Who is turning your positions red or green anyway? The *sharks* are! Barring some catastrophic event affecting a company or stock, you're making money either way. It's really more a question of how much you make rather than if you will make money. You are a winner anyway. Now, I want to be a big winner, and I'm not going to let profits sit on the table idly. I'm going to stay proactive. When a sell ripens, I'm going to sell and buy income with it.

10. *Use this strategy consistently.* Just paying a little attention, you will beat what you benchmark your portfolio to. I've benchmarked mine to SPY, an exchange-traded fund (ETF) that mimics the S&P 500 Index. I use SPY and not the index, because the ETF has expenses and trading has cost associated with it. I have brokerage costs. The index does not. Over just two months, I beat SPY by 3 percent and took my projected annual revenue to $65,000. This is a 6 percent yield over my entire portfolio. I've followed this daily, and my performance continues to pull away in total return (revenue plus appreciation). This is compelling and started me writing this book. Note that it took some time to craft this book, and my yield and portfolio changed frequently. As I wrote more, my yield continued to increase.

Risk-Management

A lot of risk-management is built into this strategy and often follows as a consequence of the strategy:

- Fundamental analysis assures continued dividend payment and likely increasing dividend payments.
- Taking profits keeps reducing the original principal paid for a position. This is then reinvested.
- Buying down into shares is done with free-trade money.
- Profits are taken quickly when the whole market is up deliriously and is highly correlated.
- If the market drops in a highly correlated movement, buy down with cheaper share prices.
- Revenue is constantly generated for you to take advantage of.
- Most of the stocks you own will have as much beta as the S&P. However, this process reduces the overall beta on your portfolio. The strategy blunts volatility.
- Lots of our companies will be increasing dividends—just one extra blessing!
- ALWAYS sell your lowest yielding shares, that is, your most expensive shares to take profits with.

Seeing, Believing, Receiving: Results and Implications

What follows is an overall picture of my portfolio at the close on 7/31/12. Present positions are as follows:

Position	Present Yield	My Yield	Discussion
WHR	2.93%	3.7%	As a consequence of buying down, I'm now taking profits as WHR is on a run.
WEA	8.13%	8.37%	Increased by buying down
WMT	2.12%	2.72%	By buying down
VOD	5.15%	7.03%	By buying down
UIL	4.63%	4.61%	Bought high and cost-averaged down; yield increases
TCAP	8.61%	8.77%	Bought down into once
TLP	7.11%	7.63%	
TOT	6.34%	6.33%	Bought slightly high compared to present price. Price change is not enough to buy down into.

Position	Present Yield	My Yield	Discussion
TEF	11.80%	9.42%	Stock tanked, and I progressively bought down into it. I feel confident that it will pay its dividend, so I've lowered my overall cost and increased yield. Now, however, my position is around $32,000. I will sell off to bring the position back to $25,000. I'll take some loss on the stock but not the portfolio, because it is already priced into the portfolio value. This $7,000 will be put to use elsewhere. Again, risk management reduced the loss compared to selling the whole position at first panic. Also, the market sharks are likely gaming it down disproportionately because of the European financial crisis. Home base is Spain. When it comes back, I'll take profits.
SYY	3.68%	3.64%	
UGT	5.75%	5.65%	
PSEC	10.98%	10.87%	
PG	3.48%	3.53%	
PBI	11.25%	10.41%	Same problem as TEF. Same action planned.
OZM	5.10%	5.04%	Stock tanked with the European crisis and I chased down. Eventually sold off half and took the loss on the stock. When the stock started rising, I came in fairly heavy, and my yield is now close to market. OZM usually has an owner distribution closer to 10%. Has now insider buying.
TAXI	7.53%	7.78%	Bought down and when it came up, took profits. Got the best of both directions.
KMP	6.15%	5.92%	
CLF	6.13%	5.16%	Similar situation to OZM. Has insider buying.

Position	Present Yield	My Yield	Discussion
			For the rest of my positions, my yield is close to or slightly better than the market. Most are having a run, and I'm taking profits progressively. My yield stays preserved when selling for a profit.
SUI	5.44%		
RLI	1.99%		Past two years paid a huge extra dividend in December
PYY	6.0%		
JQC	8.62%		
MVO	10.60%		
MSFT	2.71%		Has had great momentum, and I've sold off most of it progressively.
NTLS	7.91%		Same thing
NEE	3.38%		Sold off just about all. Had a great run.
MMP	4.85%		
MCN	9.23%		
LMT	4.47%		
LLY	4.44%		Remarkable; I had for years and it never did anything. It's having a fantastic run, and I'm taking all the capital gain off the table when it shows up!
LGCY	8.48%		
JNJ	3.52%		Same story as LLY. The pharmaceuticals all seem to be running. Hot subsector. I bought a full position of AZN with a 6% yield, as I expect to run out of LLY. This is exactly what happened to my PFE. When I sold the last shares, I was up almost 60%.
IBM	1.73%		I bought before I started completely turning over my portfolio to compound yield. I'm up 55% in the position and rather than just sitting on it, I'm happy to keep selling calls on it until I lose it. My yield is 3%.
INTC	3.5%		Bought anticipating losing IBM
HCP	4.24%		
EXC	5.36%		

Position	Present Yield	My Yield	Discussion
EXG	11.47%		
ESV	2.76%		
DDT	6.625%		
UAN	8.80		
COP	4.85%		
CMO	11.36%		
BCS.A	7.1%		
BP	4.79%		Has had a great run, and I may run out of shares. Bought COP to replace.
BGS	3.86%		
ADP	2.79%		I'll probably run out of shares also.
T	4.63%		I'll also likely lose all shares; bought VOD to replace.
AZN	6.08%		
AGNC	14.22%		
AEH	6.35%		

Disclaimer: I'm making no recommendation to own any of these. Do your own research and buy what *you* want. It's your own responsibility to grab your future.

Total of fifty-four positions. Of these fifty-four, how many yield greater than 7 percent? Nineteen, or 33 percent.

Over my entire portfolio, my estimated income is now $76,000. This equals 7.2 percent on my original principal. Is this not staggering?

Using the rule of seventy-two, the doubling time to $152,000 is ten years, provided that I keep reinvesting at 7.2 percent return annually. At fifty-four years old, I'd be able to think seriously about retiring at sixty-four. Hopeless to sixty-four is miraculous!

The likelihood of this holding up is excellent. Let's suppose that, conservatively, dividends rise at 3 percent annually: 7.2 percent minus 3 percent equals 4.2 percent. This portfolio has thirty-eight positions that yield better than that already. Thirty-eight out of fifty-four is 70.4 percent! With buying down into the remainder over time alone, the majority will get up to 4 percent. It might take a year or two. As capital gain is taken off as profit, the strategy supercharges the portfolio with free-trade money. We compound our results by buying down or opening new positions with free-trade money. This is incredibly powerful. For this portfolio to earn 7.2 percent yet have only 33 percent of the positions earning more than that—how's that possible? *Free-trade money.* Put it to use. Sell capital gain, and don't let it sit there looking good on paper as part of your "total gain." Gain is only real when it's in your pocket to buy something. Why would you not buy income? This is great investing and the best of trading. We never lose on a trade. We know how much capital gain we have before we take it. We don't gamble on market direction. We don't have to trade alongside the sharks. We give them what they want for a profit. We don't have to figure out where they are because they tell us. We just want to be there to greet them. We protect ourselves, should they not be interested in some of our stocks, by making high yield while they change their minds. It's all a game, and until now, we've been the losers. Every step of this formula has risk-management built in.

The plan is clear in what to do at every turn. Even if an occasional position turns out to be a big loser because we were lied to about fundamentals, the analysts were misled, or there was an event of catastrophic proportion, we protected ourselves by position sizing.

From what was described above, I only have to secure a return of 4.2 percent provided the dividends grow at 3 percent. The plan has multiple ways to do this, and each is risk-managed. We have to take control of retirement. There is no risk-management in a traditional 401K. I don't see how a mutual-fund manager can be effective if nearly instant information can hit the streets everywhere and people just react emotionally. There really is no time to respond rationally. Those who panic will continue to go into and out of the market following the crowd or just stay sidelined. When people decide to bail, they usually take all their money with them. How can a fund manager be prepared for this without holding enough cash back? This cash is then not in the market to advance the fund's objectives. How can the managers beat the market? The market itself is not trustable. Emotion and volatility are here to stay. The sharks are ready to take the amateur, naïve, or complacent money. I'm not going to live another "lost decade." I choose to be a Compound Yield investor. I'll make my returns honestly and consistently by providing what the other sharks want or need. There is no gaming, no lying, no cheating. There don't have to be any victims to succeed. I just see it, believe it, and receive my growing returns.

Back-Test of Compound Yield on SPY

I back-tested on SPY to see what percent correct decisions would have been made starting from the 2008 peak, then crash, then recovery to the present. I just used every quarterly dividend day rough closing price and calculated the change in price and yield one quarter to the next. Back-testing my individual holdings, I would have picked them so that I had stable dividends or increasing ones through the test period. This would have given me perfect decisions. It made more sense to back-test SPY. SPY is an ETF for the S&P 500 index. For SPY, however, the dividend changed up or down on different quarters. Our decision to buy or sell is only predicated on whether the share price was up or down enough for us to act. For individual stocks, we would not know when the dividend might change. On SPY we can see what would have happened to our yield. Basically, a right decision would occur when the share price went down and the yield went up on a particular quarter. A wrong decision would occur if price and yield moved in the same direction.

Dividend Paid Date	Dividend Paid	Closing Price	Spot Annual Yield	% Stock Price Change	Spot Change in Quarterly Yield
12/21/07	0.72	152.58	1.9%		
3/21/08	0.78	131.97	2.4%	down 13.5%	+26%
6/20/08	0.67	127.98	2.1%	down 3%	-12.5%
9/19/08	0.69	115.99	2.4%	down 9.4%	+14.3%
12/19/08	0.72	90.24	3.2%	down 22.2%	+33.3%
3/20/09	0.56	79.52	2.8%	down 12%	-12.5%
6/19/09	0.52	91.95	2.3%	up 15.6%	-17.9%
9/18/09	0.51	105.59	1.9%	up 14.8%	-17.4%
12/18/09	0.59	114.44	2.1%	up 8.4%	+10.5%
3/19/10	0.48	118.81	1.6%	up 3.8%	-23.8%
6/18/10	0.53	103.22	2.1%	down 13%	+31.25%
9/17/10	0.60	118.49	2.0%	up 15%	-4.8%
12/17/10	0.65	125.75	2.1%	up 6.1%	+5%
3/18/11	0.55	132.59	1.7%	up 5.4%	-19%
6/17/11	0.63	131.97	1.9%	down 0.5%	+12%
9/16/11	0.62	113.15	2.2%	down 14.2%	+15.8%
12/16/11	0.77	125.50	2.5%	up 11%	+13.6%
3/16/12	0.61	140.81	1.7%	up 12.2%	-32%
6/15/12	0.69	136.11	2.0%	down 3.3%	+17.6%

So from the above: The spot annual yield is simply calculated as the dividend paid X 4 (four quarters a year) and then divided by the share price for that day. The % Stock Price change is a comparison from one date to the preceding date. From 12/21/07 to 3/21/08, the price change was calculated: 131.97 minus 152.58 equal -20.61. This then divided by 152.58 comes to 0.135 then by 100 gives us the % change or -13.5%.

Similarly, I did this for the Spot Annual Yield: 2.4% minus 1.9% equals 0.5%. This divided by 1.9% equals Spot Change in Quarterly yield of 0.26 X 100 or +26%. In this manner, the chart reflects the performance of SPY quarter over quarter. Each date's results were generated this way.

- 3/08: Stock dropped 13.5 percent and yield increased 26 percent; would have bought.
- 6/08: Stock dropped 3 percent and yield dropped by 12.5 percent; probably would not have done anything because the general rule is not to sell or buy unless greater than one year's dividend yield.
- 9/08: Stock dropped by 9.4 percent and yield increased 14.3 percent; would have bought.
- 12/08: Stock dropped by 22.2 percent and yield increased 33.3 percent; would have bought.
- 3/09: Stock dropped 12 percent and yield dropped 12.5 percent; would have bought and would have been more or less break-even.
- 6/09: Stock up by 15.6 percent and yield decreased by 17.8 percent; would have sold.
- 9/09: Stock up by 14.8 percent and yield down 14.3 percent; would have sold.
- 12/09: Stock up 8.4 percent and yield up 10.5 percent; would have sold at slight disadvantage.
- 3/10: Stock up 3.8 percent and yield down 23.8 percent; would have sold.

- 6/10: Stock down 13 percent and yield up 31.25 percent; would have bought.
- 9/10: Stock up 15 percent and yield down 4.8 percent; would have sold.
- 12/10: Stock up 6.1 percent and yield up 5 percent; would have sold.
- 3/11: Stock up 5.4 percent and yield down 19 percent; would have sold.
- 6/11: Stock down 0.5 percent and yield up 12 percent; probably would have done nothing.
- 9/11: Stock down 14.2 percent and yield up 15.8 percent; would have bought.
- 12/11: Stock up 11 percent and yield up 13.6 percent; would have sold more or less break even.
- 3/12: Stock up 12.2 percent and yield down 32 percent; would have sold.
- 6/12: Stock down 3.3 percent and yield up 17.6 percent; probably would have done nothing.

Of my decisions, twelve out of eighteen, or 67 percent, were clearly correct. Five out of eighteen, or 27 percent, did nothing or broke even. One out of eighteen, or 6 percent, was just slightly wrong. Correct decisions occur when the stock price moves opposite to the change in yield. Wrong decisions have the stock price and yield moving in the same direction. Here, our overall win, did nothing (neither loss nor gain) or essentially break even trades back-tested on SPY, comes out to 94 percent and one trade, just slightly bad, represents 6 percent. The compound yield strategy would have been consistent and very successful back-tested through the Great Recession.

Tremendous!

Growing with the Plan and Some Lessons Learned

For this next part, I thought it might be eye-popping to go through what I did as though we were doing it together. For this purpose, I've adapted my e-mail records to my brokerage team at Scott and Stringfellow in chronological order. They run from 6/28/12 through 8/6/12.

6/28/12
Mathematics of Interest

The process is unfolding, and success is showing itself in a big way. My general principles are outlined as the "5Bs."

John, just to check on strategy, I did some math:

Before the market start today, I printed off the portfolio.

Total cost of assets: $1,088,044.02.

Total cost of 5 letter ticket symbols: $134,524.92. I included PRPFX, PARSX, ODMAX, SGENX, KAUAX, HSTRX.

This morning's value $125,115.88.

$125,115.88 - $134,524.92 = -$9,409.04. $9,409.04 divided by $134,524.92 = down 7%.

$1,088,044.02 - $134,524 = $953,519.10 is the cost of portfolio stocks and remaining options.

As of this AM, the value of the portfolio was $1,067,084.57.

$1,067,084.57 - $125,115.88 = $941,968.69 equals the AM value of stocks and options.

$941,968.69 - $953,519.10 = -$11,550.41 This is the loss on stocks and options.

-$11,550.41 divided by $953,519.10 = -1.2%

So, on the mutual funds, we're down 7% and the stocks and options are down just 1.2%. Additionally, the mutual funds do not participate in any income for the portfolio.

This is where it gets even more enlightening. The present annual income expectation is now up to $54,000.

On the whole portfolio this represents: $54,000 divided by $1,088,044.02 = 4.96% annually.

That's fairly impressive—BUT, if we do this calculation on just the part of portfolio that is generating it, namely stocks, options, TAKING PROFITS AND BUYING INCOME, we have:

$54,000 divided by $953,519.10 = 5.7%.

So: mutual funds are down 7% and no contribution to income.

THE STRATEGY is down 1.2% and generating $54,000 of income annually.

John, I hope you didn't get hurt falling out of your chair. Holy cow! and we did this in a few months in a volatile market.

5Bs of the strategy:
- Buy the best stocks you can find with a good/great yield and the fundamentals are there to protect the future dividend payments.
- Bait the market and have the sharks find you i.e. you are seeing green on the Web page.
- Be kind and feed the sharks. Don't leave food on the table; turn capital gain into income.
- Believe the strategy. It is emotionless. It tells you what to do. If you're up 1X annual dividend, sell enough shares to capture the profit. FEED THE SHARKS, THEY WERE KIND ENOUGH TO TELL YOU WHERE THEY ARE. If you're down on a stock that has excellent fundamentals so the dividend is secure, BUY and increase your yield on net asset value. Whether the stock is RED or GREEN is the consequence of the SHARKS. FEED THEM!! The SHARKS TRADE. THEY DO NOT INVEST. The strategy trades to buy income. It

cannot lose on a trade because it is selling GREEN. Sell high (GREEN), buy low (RED).
- Be steadfast and execute consistently.

Additionally, if dividends grew at an average of 3%, after 6 years (I picked because I'll be 59 and one-half) the $54,000 alone becomes $64,478.82.

I cannot imagine a safer approach to reach retirement.

John, you're probably wondering what's going on with me. Well, kids are at camp and wife is the camp nurse. It's just the dogs and me.

As always, I appreciate you/your help and advice. Bob Nag . . . MD

P.S. SPY from when I started with Scott and Stringfellow to present day is down 2.4%. This strategy provides portfolio growth and accelerating income with risk management built in. Pretty blow away, don't you think?

6/29/12
Taking Profits

You'll notice that my profits are huge. This is because I'm trading over short intervals. I'm not fighting against any long-term trend, just paying attention to when I seem to be up roughly equal to the annual dividend or so. By selling enough shares just to capture profits, most of the whole position remains. During this early process, I don't have to worry about losing or having to replace the income from the shares sold for this purpose. I plan to buy much higher-income-yielding stocks.

John, all markets are up deliriously so. Take profits as planned.

Sell all of MPH, KFT
Take profits on:
PFE I'm up 32%
MSFT I'm up 13%
WMT I'm up 18%
WHR hasn't been green for days. I'm up 3.5%.
UAN I'm up 10%
T I'm up 23%
ADP I'm up 13%
LLY I'm up 9%
NEE I'm up 9%
DDD I'm up 11%
JNJ I'm up 4%
LMT I'm up 19.4%
EXPE up 44% !!!

Thanks

7/5/12
Taking Profits Off the Table

Because I'm starting to see the likelihood of substantial trading in this manner, I start calculating how many shares to sell on each position. For each individual trade, the number of shares sold is small compared to what remains invested. I thought I would make it easier and quicker to execute through my broker, which it has. Additionally, this really should be my responsibility anyway.

> John, Julie, I've done my calculations and want to take profits off the table
>
> PFE I'm up 30.5%. Sell 25 shares.
> NEE I'm up 8.6%. Sell 12 shares.
> MSFT I'm up 14%. Sell 75 shares.
> TLP I'm up 8.8%. Sell 50 shares.
> WMT I'm up 21.7%. Sell 20 shares.
> SUI I'm up 7.2%. Sell 9 shares.
> TOT I'm up 6.6%. Sell 14 shares.
> DDD I'm up 19.1%. Sell 45 shares.
> UAN I'm up 10.3%. Sell 75 shares.
> COP I'm up 5%. Sell 14 shares.
> T I'm up 23.4%. Sell 76 shares.
> BP I'm up 6.6%. Sell 22 shares.
> ADP I'm up 15.4%. Sell 32 shares.
> DOLE I'm up 6.7%. Sell 95 shares.
> LLY I'm up 14.5%. Sell 90 shares.
> JNJ I'm up 5.8%. Sell 30 shares.
> EXPE I'm up 46.7%. Sell 25 shares.
> XLS I'm up 5.7%. Sell 45 shares.
> WHR I'm up 11%. Sell 47 shares.
> JQC I'm up 5.7%. Sell 156 shares.

Total profits almost $30,000, which equals about 2.7% of portfolio.

Thanks Bob Nag . . . MD

7/6/12
Position Sizing

Great trade day. I'm opening a new full position from profits alone. None of my original capital is in this position. Believe me, I'm excited.

> John, Julie. GREAT day to buy. Working on position sizes to $25,000 each.
>
> $77,000 cash on hand
>
> BUY TAXI 550 shares for about $6,000
> BUY MMP 30 shares for about $2,000
> BUY UTG 130 shares for about $3,500
> BUY TCAP 175 shares for about $4,000
> Buy TOT 120 shares for about $5,400
> Buy UAN 340 shares for about $8,500
> BUY CMO 430 shares for about $8,000
> BUY AGNC 150 shares for about $5,000
> BUY ANH 1500 shares for about $5,000
>
> Totals to about $47,000

New position Lockheed Martin LMT $86.59 x 290 shares
= about $25,000

Pare down on PG. Sell 100 shares for about $6,000.
Pare down on CLF. Sell 85 shares for about $4,000.

$47,000 + $25,000 - $10,000 = $62,000

$77,000 - $62,000 should leave in cash about $15,000

Thanks, Bob Nag . . . MD

7/9/12
Sizing Positions

Pretty huge sums moving around here. This impresses me. It certainly shows my conviction.

John, Julie, just mainly sizing positions to $25,000.

SELL JNJ 120 shares for about $8,000
SELL KMP 145 shares for about $12,000
SELL ESV 275 shares for $14,000
SELL all HIG for about $30,000 has too poor a dividend and we're down a lot
SELL all XYL for about $5,000
SELL all XLS for about $6,700
SELL SYY 240 shares for about $7,000
TOTALS to about $82,700

BUY UTG 370 shares for about $10,000

BUY TCAP 430 shares for about $10,000

BUY TLP 230 shares for about $8,000

BUY TOT 225 shares for about $10,000

BUY AGNC 290 shares for about $10,000

BUY ANH 590 shares for about $4,000

BUY new position AEGON 7.5% preferred for $25,000

TOTALS to about $77,000

$82,000 - $77,000 + $15,000 (which is in account now) = $20,000 cash left in account

I'll call in AM to confirm. I appreciate all the help. Once I'm as far as I can go with sizing, the frequency of trades should drop way back. I'll try to take profits all on one day and buy down into positions or buy a new one on another day. Will try to make simpler.

Thanks, Bob Nag . . . MD

7/12/12
Trades

Same thing. Working rapidly to size each position.

John, Julie, want to:

SELL PFE 18 shares I'm up 28%

SELL MSFT 43 shares up 8.9%

SELL NTLS 30 shares up 7.3%
SELL NEE 10 shares up 7.6%
SELL TLP 55 shares up 7.6%
SELL WMT 17 shares up 24%
SELL WHR 45 shares up 12.3%
SELL DDD 15 shares up 7%
SELL BP 18 shares up 5.8%
SELL T 60 shares up 22%
SELL ADP 25 shares up 14%
SELL LLY 86 shares up 16.34%
SELL JNJ 24 shares up 6.8%
SELL EXPE 14 shares up 38%
SELL JQC 190 shares up 7.3%

TOTALS TO: $21,318.95

BUY PSEC 585 shares for $6,400
BUY MMP 110 shares for $8,000
BUY INTC 257 shares for $7,000

TOTALS $21,400

Should leave in cash in portfolio $19,000

Thanks Bob Nag . . . MD

$21,318.95 divided by $1,070,000 = about 2% of starting portfolio value.

Addendum: Positions are just slightly down this AM, so I think we can get it done. If we're a little shorter than calculations, then buy what we can of Intel INTC.

7/16/12
Sizing Trades, Two New Positions

Buying down into a position. I've done my research. I'm buying down to increase yield.

John, Julie, good morning.
SELL all HSTRX for about $16,500
SELL all STT for about $17,700 dividend too low and stock seems unpredictable
Present cash in portfolio $17,498

TRADES:
SELL PFE up 30.5% sell 15 shares about $330
SELL MMP up 5.3% sell 17 shares about $1,286
SELL MSFT up 9.3% sell 41 shares about $1,204
SELL JQC up 7.97% sell 188 shares for $1,769
SELL NTLS up 7.3% sell 27 shares for $554
Sell NEE up 9.2% sell 10 shares for $725
SELL TLP up 5.6% sell 38 shares for $1,340
SELL WMT up 25.4% sell 15 shares for $1,081
SELL WHR up 15.17% sell 50 shares for $3,127
SELL WEA up 8.9% sell 32 shares for $513
SELL DDD up 7.1% sell 15 shares for $482
SELL BP up 7.7% sell 22 shares for $906

SELL T up 22% sell 48 shares for $1,690

SELL ADP up 14.9% sell 23 shares $1,307

SELL LLY up 17.2% sell 77 shares $3,323

SELL JNJ up 7.9% sell 25 shares $1,751

SELL EXPE up 38% sell 10 shares for $452

TOTALS about $21,840

BUY VOD $25,000 $25.59 buy 977 shares pays dividend 5.21%

BUY UIL $25,000 $37.44 buy 668 shares pays dividend yield 4.62%

$16,000 + $17,700 + $17,498 + $21,840 - $25,000 - $25,000 = remaining cash of about $23,038

Also, PBI is down 7%. Will buy down into $1,737 buy 125 shares.

Market may tank a good bit by end of week, so I'll ride out on my puts for a couple of days.

Thanks again, I'll call to confirm.

7/20/12
More Sizing

My winners keep running until I run out of shares. Certainly a nice problem to have. I've bought down into TEF and eventually I'll sell all of it when it suspends its dividend. It's my first loser. Importantly, it comes as no surprise. The system identified it as an at-risk position, as I would buy down into it again. This shows me that I just need to be emotionless. The analysts got it wrong. The fundamentals were not what they were promoted to be. That's why sizing is important, as is diversification.

John, Julie—

Good morning, just a little today. Some sizing.

SELL all of DOLE for about $12,000
SELL all PFE for $926. What a great ride. Sad to see it go, but was nice to watch it leave progressively for profit!
SELL all EXPE for $903. Same feelings.
TOTAL about $13,800

Sizing:
BUY PBI 185 shares for $2500
BUY OZM 290 shares for $2000
BUY TEF 425 shares for $5300
BUY CLF 45 shares for $2100
TOTAL of about $11,900

Could you check web page? UTG listed twice. Second listing is "UTG—" Not sure what this means. Has been there for days.

Also, close out puts on S&P and the QQQs.

Thanks. I'm trying to force myself to not take off profits until Web page/account clears through settlement dates. Thanks. Bob Nag . . . MD

7/23/12
Homework Weekend

Stocks that I bought down into now have an upturn, and I take that profit off the table on those for the first time. Also, I'm starting to really pay attention to yield. I also check what happened overnight before executing by looking at the foreign indexes and the S&P futures. I don't like big surprises.

Did some homework on weekend. Put a few hours into it and it was fun!

SELLS
Sell WHR I'm up 24.12% sell 54 shares to take profit about $3600
Sell WEA up 4% sell 61 shares for $1004
Sell WMT up 24% sell 9 shares for $650
sell TLP up 7.7% sell 46 shares for $1620
Sell DDD up 13.3% sell 21 shares for $730
Sell SUI up 10.1% sell 10 shares for $450
Sell JQC up 8.1% sell 163 shares for $1520
Sell NTLS up 6% sell 19 shares for $390
Sell NEE up 11% sell 10 shares for $720
Sell MSFT up 12% sell 42 shares for $1270

Sell TAXI up 5.5% sell 116 shares for $1320. First time up for TAXI.

Sell MMP up 7.05% sell 20 shares for $1600

Sell LLY up 18% sell 56 shares for $2400. What a superstar. For 15 years I had it, did nothing.

Sell JNJ up 8.1% sell 22 shares for $1600

Sell EXC up 5% sell 14 shares for $600

Sell ESV up 2.8% sell 14 shares for $750

Sell UAN up 6.5% sell 60 shares for $1500

Sell COP up 5.4% sell 15 shares for $850

Sell BP up 9.4% sell 23 shares for $950

Sell ADP up 13% sell 15 shares for $850

Sell T up 22% sell 31 shares for $1000

TOTAL: about $25,374

Present projected annual income on original principal of $1,070,0000 = 7.3%

At 7.3%, I think we should take profits on the preferreds

Sell DDT up 32.4% sell 180 shares for $4,500

Sell BCS.A up 26.8% sell 158 shares for $3,900

Sell BAC.J up 27.3% sell 160 shares for $4,000

TOALS: $12,400

BUYS

Buy LGCY Legacy Reserves LP $27.95 7.94% dividend yield; steady and increasing dividend; strong fundamentals to secure dividend. $25,000 divided by $27.95 = buy 894 shares.

Buy SYY I'm down 3% $722.91 $28.87 buy 25 shares
Buy UTG down by 3.84% $972.73 $25.66 buy 38 shares
Buy INTC down 3.3% $573.97 $25.52 buy 22 shares

Total spent $25,000 + $723 + $972 + $574 = $27,269
Available: $21,400 + $12,400 = $33,800
Difference available $6,531
Cash in account about $8,000

Want to open small position on RLI. Property and casualty insurance $63.03 $10,000 buy 158 shares. Thompson Reuter positive, Smart Consensus long. Dividend about 2.8% but last 2 years, special huge dividend in Nov/Dec past 2 years making overall yield greater than 8%. Regular dividend increasing for years.

As of close Friday, portfolio up 3.3% and SPY up 0.26% from when I started with Scott and Stringfellow. Difference of +3.04% and portfolio income projected annual of $75,000. I think we're making progress.

Thanks, Bob Nag . . . MD

7/27/12

Modest Changes

I'm mainly paying attention to a truer profit margin by accounting for share dividend loss. Also, I'm paying attention to remaining free cash.

> John, Jeff, and Julie. Good morning. We've reached a point where I think trade days will be less often and fewer changes.
>
> SELLS
>
> Sell WHR up $2762.08 $66.90 sell 41 shares I'm up 23% - 7% dividend = 16% profit to increase income with
>
> Sell WMT up $566.16 $73.67 sell 7 shares up 26% - 2.5 dividend = 23.5% profit
>
> Sell SUI up $370.51 $46.00 = sell 8 shares up 9.3% - 5% = 4.3% profit
>
> Sell NEE up $683.00 $70.72 = sell 10 shares up 11.5% - 3.6% dividend = 7.9% profit
>
> Sell MSFT up $794.62 $29.16 = sell 27 shares up 8.4% - 2.2% = 6.2% profit
>
> Sell LLY $1929.63 $43.61 = 44 shares up 16.2% - 2.2% = 14% profit
>
> Sell JNJ $1433.87 $68.74 = 21 shares up 8.3% - 3.6% = 4.7% profit
>
> Sell DDD $519.57 $34.18 = sell 15 shares up 11% - 0 = 11% profit

Sell BP $712 $40.91 = sell 17 shares up 7.9% - 4.81% = 3.09% profit

Sell MMP $1832.90 $77.72 = sell 23 shares up 9.1% - 4.54% = 4.56% profit

Sell ADP $764.82 $56.52 sell 13 shares up 12% - 2.85% = 9.15% profit

Sell T $1047.45 $36.30 = sell 29 shares up 25.4% - 4.98% = 20.42% profit

TOTALS to $13,416.61

BUY

Buy PBI $3318.06 $13.06 = 255 shares to buy

Buy LGCY $884.72 $26.58 = 33 shares

Buy INTC $5,000 $25.50 = 196 shares

Should leave about $3,000 cash

Present cash about $8,000

Thanks, Bob Nag . . . MD

7/30/12
Sticking to My Rules

I have my first indication that I'll have to size down a position that I bought down into as the market climbs.

John, Julie—

The market is delirious and really correlated. Time to take profits.

SELL

Sell WHR up 26.3% present yield 2.92% sell 37 shares for about $2500

Sell WMT up 27.7% 2.13% sell 7 shares for $500

Sell DDD up 21.9% 0% sell 25 shares $900

Sell TLP up 10.2% 6.98% sell 55 shares $2000

Sell JQC up 8.9% 8.59% sell 166 shares $1500

Sell NEE up 13.1% 3.38% sell 10 shares $700

Sell MSFT up 10.6% 2.69% sell 31 shares $900

Sell MMP up 9.3% 4.83% sell 22 shares $1700

Sell LMT up 4.43% 4.43% sell 12 shares $1100. First time to winner circle.

Sell LLY up 18.2% 4.42% sell 42 shares $1800

Sell JNJ up 9.6% 3.51% sell 22 shares $1500

Sell HCP up 5.8% 4.2% sell 30 shares $1400. First time to winner circle.

Sell EXC up 5.2% 5.3% sell 14 shares $550

Sell ESV up 7.4% 2.75% sell 35 shares $1900

Sell BP up 9.6% 4.62% sell 20 shares $850

Sell BGS up 4.1% 3.86% sell 36 shares $1000. First time to winner circle.

Sell ADP up 15% 2.74% sell 14 shares $800

Sell T up 28.4% 4.74% sell 25 shares $900

TOTAL of about $22,500

BUY This is where I have to stay true to the plan. Did do my research and will bite the bullet on TEF and CLF.

Buy TEF 129 shares for $1500

> Buy UTG 33 shares for $850
> Buy PBI 230 shares for $3000. 90% institutionally owned. Being shorted. See no bad news.
> Buy OXM 320 shares for $2300
> Buy CLF 152 shares for $6000. Price to tangible value close to 1. It has gotten slaughtered and has insider buying. My hedge-type fund subscription editor says buy and will buy down if price drops further.
> TOTAL about $13,650
>
> For this buying, I'm just trying to keep each position around $25,000. I'm a little heavy with PBI. Probably miscalculated a little along the way. Insider buying has been big and I'll be quick to take profits to get size to $25,000.
>
> As always, thanks, Bob Nag . . . MD

Unfortunately, I make an error on a trade symbol, and it costs me about $230 to undo. I meant OZM and I typed OXM, and I have to send a follow-up e-mail:

> John, I screwed up ticker symbol. My intention was to buy down into OZM $2300. I typed in e-mail OXM. I missed it. Let's sell OXM and buy OZM. My painful mistake. Thanks Bob Nag . . . MD

8/12/12
Need to Sell TEF

Selling whole position on TEF. By buying down with free-trade money, I reduce my original principal in the position and overall lose less. I really do not have to sweat it, as the loss is already accounted for in my total portfolio value. Selling today or any other day won't change that. No need for emotion. Get rid of your losers.

> John, Julie, good morning. Need to sell all of TEF. Has suspended dividends for rest of the year. This is fairly huge. Pays dividends only twice a year. I would have been due over $2,000 December 2012. Let's buy Bristol-Myers Squibb. BMY. It's having a good run like JNJ and LLY, which I've been taking profits on regularly. Probably need another Pharma anyway. Pays 3.8% yield. Fundamentals very good. Stock Scouter rates as 9 of 10. Payout ratio 64%. Let's buy another $10,000 DDD. Really an incredible technology and has been great to take profits on. TEF down to $24,000. We have plenty of cash in account. TEF down 20% so hit my mental stop-loss anyway.
>
> Thanks,
> Bob Nag . . . MD

8/6/12

Trades and Sizing

Now I'm really paying attention to calculating the annual lost revenue on shares sold for profit-taking. I account for it so I can be sure that I buy enough yield on a new position or old position that I don't lose ground on my portfolio's annual yield. This is for the first set of trades today.

> John, Jeff, Julie, good morning. Friday was a good day. Will need to take profits. [Profit capture cost refers to the annual revenue we would have expected on the shares we sold to capture profit.]

SELL

Symbol	Amount	Price	Sell Shares	Profit Capture Cost	Present Yield	Position Up
WHR	$2191.81	$69.54	32	$65.54	2.99%	31.51%
TLP	$1673.68	$36.60	46	$116.99	6.99%	9.2%
TOT	$2239.75	$47.73	50	$142.00	6.34%	9.2%
DDD	$1304.03	$38.50	34	$0.00	0%	9.6%
JQC	$1727.93	$9.43	183	$148.08	8.57%	10.9%
NEE	$653.33	$70.87	9	$22.34	3.42%	14.4%
MSFT	$836.91	$29.75	264	$22.93	2.74%	10.7%
MMP	$1452.95	$77.78	19	$69.45	4.78%	8.6%
LLY	$1522.10	$44.15	35	$68.80	4.52%	17.5%
JNJ	$1310.38	$69.12	19	$46.65	3.56%	9%
ESV	$2451.35	$55.66	44	$67.17	2.74%	10.2%
BP	$636.20	$41.03	16	$30.60	4.81%	8.4%
BGS	$1250.38	$28.31	44	$48.26	3.86%	5.2%
ADP	$643.88	$56.93	11	$18.22	2.83%	13.9%
T	$770.90	$37.58	21	$36.15	4.69%	30%

TOTAL $20,665.58

BUY

SUI 5.33% yield will need to size up to $25,000 - $3662.69 = $21,337.31 $47.29 buy 451 shares

UTG 5.81% yield $769.31 $25.80 will need to buy 30 shares

PSEC 11.11% yield $568.95 $10.97 will need to buy 52 shares

LGCY 8.54% yield $1228.85 $26.24 will need to buy 47 shares

KMP 6.16% yield $724.95 $79.83 will need to buy 9 shares

ANH 10.93% yield $716.79 $6.59 will need to buy 109 shares

TOTALS to about $25,346

Cash in account about $11,000 + $20,665.58 - $25,346 = ABOUT $6,250 left

John, I expect less trade days. Because the yields are good on our holdings, to compensate for the shares I sell annual dividend loss, I need to reinvest at a minimum of 4.8% return. As time goes on, this minimum will climb further and I'll have to be picky about taking profits.

Thanks, Bob Nag . . . MD

8/6/12

For My Broker's Eyes Only

I really want to buy VNR. I push the limit on when to take profits. This really is a proof-of-concept of the system, and a successful one at that.

> John, in all seriousness, this is for your eyes only. This is the second trade set I want to do. I'll send the first set to you in the morning. I'll have to check the futures market first to be sure there are no surprises. This second set will tightly test the Compound Yield concept. What follows may surprise you as it provides absolute proof of concept. Up till now, we've taken high profits of 8% to 20% or more essentially by spot trading each position. We took off profits by selling just enough shares. These shares do have a relative loss associated with them, namely the income their loss represents annually. It can be calculated. We've automatically compensated for this because our profit margins have been so high such that the portfolio overall's yield increased progressively to $77,000. When I sold TEF because it suspended its dividend payment (which, by the way, was done with no emotion and you know I've read everything I could get my hands on for weeks now), this really slammed my annual income to $73,600. This certainly was eye-popping to me and pushed me to this next level. Put your seat belt on!!

Focusing on yield again provides the answer. The set-up is as follows: CLD/profit-taking reflects the calculated cost of annual dividend loss on the shares sold to capture profits. Adjusted profit is the total trade profit minus the CLD/profit taking.

SELL SHARES OF:

Ticker Symbol	Share Price	Position Cost	I'm Up	$Amount Up	Present Yield	CLD/ Profit Taking	Adjusted Profit
WEA	$16.26	$23,779.70	3.03%	$724.12	8%	$57.93	$666.19
VOD	$29.71	$25,147.50	3.4%	$848.72	5%	$42.44	$806.28
TCAPP	$36.60	$18,273.32	2.7%	$494.98	8.6%	$42.57	$452.41
PG	$65.50	$25,475.60	2.8%	$724.40	3.43%	$24.85	$699.55
PYY	$24.77	$25,611.54	6.4%	$1635.46	6%	$98.13	$1537.33
MFA	$8.11	$24,552.00	2.4%	$589.00	11.34%	$66.79	$522.21
TAXI	$11.26	$22,728.04	4.3%	$972.55	7.46%	$72.56	$899.99
LMT	$89.39	$23,983.03	3.6%	$867.39	4.47%	$38.77	$828.62
HCP	$46.43	$23,192.00	4.1%	$951.60	4.92%	$41.92	$909.68
EXG	$8.60	$45,053.48	3.7%	$1679.14	11.35%	$190.58	$1488.56
UAN	$24.60	$22,000.71	4%	$877.29	9.28%	$81.41	$795.88
COP	$55.71	$14,433.00	4.9%	$706.67	4.74%	$33.50	$673.17
AEH	$25.35	$24,689.00	2.7%	$661.00	10%	$66.10	$594.90
NTLS (sell all)				$5,467.26		$631.51	$4835.75
Totals				$17,199.58		$1489.06	$15,710.52

*We bought NTLS with Free Trade money

Let's see what yield we are "losing" on the adjusted profit: $1489.06 divided by $15,710.52 x 100 = 9.48% I chose using adjusted profit rather than gross profit because it builds in a little margin to be sure we do better than break even.

I really want to buy VNR Vanguard Natural Resources. Yield 8.78% P/E 12.9 tremendous fundamentals to assure the dividend payment and analysts are very positive.

We have something to fix here to make us not lose ground on our portfolio's yield. With the present overall trade, 9.5% dividend loss occurs with the sale of shares. We're doing the trade to start a new great position with a yield of 8.78%. I believe it will be a great one to take profits on and then buy down into to increase yield.

The fix: We need to enter the position with $15,710.52 x 9.5/8.78 = $16,998.85. We're $16,998.85 - $15,710.52 = $1,288.33 short. We should have this in the cash account. This cash is free trade cash. It is free and clear profit.

Monday AM, I'd like to execute the above and start a new position with VNR at $17,000 or less if our trades above come in a little short since these calculations were done Sunday.

John, this is unbelievable. My portfolio yield will climb just a little and I'll have a whole new position that contains NONE of my original principal at 8.78% or $1,492.60 income annually from here on out. Look how little percent-wise we had to let our holdings rise!!

This is why I don't want to let profits sit unattended. A hundred of these trade days would produce $100,000 income annually at that point. How long will I need to do this? 3 years? 5 years? These are pretty short times compared to 23 years to produce an overall 20% total return. I put in $800K of the million dollar portfolio. That averages to less than 1% a year. That's why I say traditional mutual fund 401K plans are doomed to fail. It's a traders market. This is our edge. The vast majority of private sector employees who do not have a defined pension are going to come up terribly short and will have paid for their public counterparts all their work lives. There has to be a way we can help them.

Thanks, Bob

In looking back on things, I did a tremendous amount of trading over a short time. I never had to lose on a trade, because the outcome was known in advance. It was profit-taking, and I used it to keep buying income.

Bottom Line: A Little Rehash from a Different Perspective

My express purpose is to duplicate the benefit of a defined-benefit pension in a 401K retirement plan. Compound Yield is a strategy that focuses on yield and makes decisions based on preserving or increasing the overall yield of a retirement portfolio. The basic structure is to invest in quality stocks or other securities to produce high return. Income generated is reinvested to increase yield or to start new positions. Capital gain is monitored for each position and is taken off the table as profit. Subsequent reinvestment of this "free trade" money to buy down into positions or start new ones compounds the benefit of dividend income by further increasing yield. A specific set of rules is adhered to in accomplishing this. Overall growth of the portfolio will likely follow consequent to these decisions. However, growth is a secondary benefit and is not our primary focus.

Ideally, we would like to generate enough retirement income so an individual retiree can have a nearly "hands off" approach. The traditional 401K mutual-fund portfolio has little likelihood of producing enough income to retire on. Results have been pitiful during the "lost decade." At least ten years have been lost, and the likelihood of recouping is poor. It is reasonable, given today's market conditions, to expect that the next ten years will be no better. Today's conditions markedly favor trading versus long-term investing. A new investment strategy is therefore needed. The only thing *real* is income received. It must be compounded. Traditional concepts of growth or growing the portfolio are as imaginary as the value of your house before the crash. Growth is, in fact, capital gain that could be captured and put to work compounding yield to increase income. Traditional thought requires that annual retirement income should be no more than 4 percent of the retirement invested nest egg. This is felt to be safe because that is the income expected by dividend return such that the loss of shares is minimized. Loss of shares is obviously detrimental and will result in nest-egg depletion. This circumstance then becomes a question of, "Run out of money, or death first?" For example, $60,000 retirement income translates into a nest egg of at least 1.5 million dollars. Even more will be needed to account for cost-of-living increases. Is that at all realistic? The unfairness of public-service defined-benefit pensions is obvious and extreme. The Compound Yield focus is growth of income, rather than growth of the portfolio to take income from. For a million-dollar portfolio, 4 percent is $40,000/year. Twice that would be needed for $80,000. Three times that would be needed for $120,000. A strategy that focuses on increasing yield is much more likely to succeed.

A net yield of 8 percent on a million-dollar portfolio would serve us better than relying on hoped-for growth to get 4 percent on a two-million-dollar portfolio. Any bad year prolongs the date of retirement. Any bad year could destroy retirement. The Compound Yield strategy is a powerful, logical, simple, and methodical path to consistent results.

The Compound Yield process is an extraordinarily defensive one, as can be seen best in the following scenario: For each of my trade days, the profits were often at a minimum of $20,000. Let's say we invested all of this in a secure stock that will never fail to pay a 5 percent dividend in my lifetime. That translates to $1,000/year for the rest of my life. Five such trade days would be $5,000/year for life. If I did a hundred trade days, that becomes $100,000 annually. That could be a comfortable retirement. I've had four such trade days in less than a month. Let's just say I could continue to do this two or three times a month, or just twenty-five times a year. That $100,000 could be achievable in four to five years. Well, this might be a little delirious, but still—holy cow!

The problem is that any single stock in any market condition may not be able to deliver on this promise. The Compound Yield formula is precisely designed to protect and enhance yield. Yield is therefore the necessary focus. By compounding yield, we are building in a protective margin. My present account has an estimated annual income of $77,000. On my original principal of $1,070,000, this is 7.2 percent. My present margin of protection is 2.2 percent (5 percent plus 2.2 percent equals 7.2 percent) over my entire portfolio. Because we are reinvesting capital gain and portfolio income consistently, the likelihood of each trade day producing $20,000 increases over time because we've added shares. The more shares, the more income, and the more opportunity to take profits on our positions and add some along the way (diversification). Protection, protection, protection. We are only interested in high-income stocks that the fundamentals can confidently assure paying and hopefully increasing dividends. More protection. Whether the stock price goes up or down, we have a clear plan that enhances protection. If we take off profits, even just once, and a position goes bad, we can never lose our entire principal. The more free-trade money we pour into a position, even less of the original principal is at risk should the position sour. We further protect ourselves by sizing each position to 2.5 percent of the portfolio. Protection. Whether the market goes up or down, we have a plan. Protection. We don't have to guess what the market sharks want because they tell us. Protection. If a shark loses interest in a stock, it's no big deal. We keep buying down until the sharks decide to game it up again. It's all a game, but we're playing back hard, and we never lose on our trades *ever*. As a freebie, dividends increase over time at 3 to 6 percent or more. To me, it's just a little extra gift from God to tell me that Compound Yield is an unlocked secret manifestation of His perfection and infinite generosity. I did have to see it to use it.

Volatility Discussion: Some Surprises

For this part, I'd like to show you volatility management. You may find this surprising and a little hard to believe. What I thought I should do is a day-over-day analysis. Recall that my comparison benchmark is SPY. When I transferred my 401K in April 2011 to my present broker, my cash value was $1,070,000. SPY closed at $136.11. The analysis is as follows:

	SPY	Account Value
April 2010	$136.11	$1,070,000
AM 7/20/12	$137.73 up 1.19%	$1,111,420.80 up 3.87%
AM 7/23/12	$136.47 down 0.91%	$1,105,473.86 down 0.54%
AM 7/24/12	$134.61 down 1.36%	$1,098,123.56 down 0.66%
AM 7/25/12	$133.93 down 0.51%	$1,088,349.92 down 0.89%
AM 7/26/12	$135.60 up 1.25%	$1,087,007.61 down 0.12%
AM 7/27/12	$136.17 up 0.42%	$1,097,553.41 up 0.97%
AM 7/30/12	$138.68 up 1.84%	$1,110,383.62 up 1.17%
AM 7/31/12	$138.68 up +0	$1,110,431.65 down -0
AM 8/1/12	$137.71 down 0.7%	$1,111,507.52 up +0

	SPY	Account Value
AM 8/2/12	$137.59 down -0	$1,110,223.45 down 0.5%
AM 8/3/12	$136.64 down 0.7%	$1,104,539.00 down 0.5%
AM 8/6/12	$139.35 up 2.0%	$1,117,977.62 up 1.22%
AM 8/7/12	$140.08 up 0.5%	$1,118,507.97 up +0

Where SPY is now: $140.08 - $136.11 divided by 136.11 x 100 = up 2.9%

Where my portfolio is now: $1,118,507.97 - $1,070,000 divided by $1,070,000 x 100 = up 4.53%

Let's just separate out the percent changes and compare side by side. Starting with 7/23/12 compared to 7/20/12 and from there, day over preceding day as a percent change either positive or negative with SPY being the left column and the right, my portfolio.

SPY	My Portfolio
-0.91	-0.54
-1.36	-0.66
-0.51	-0.89
+1.25	-0.12
+0.42	+0.97
+1.84	+1.17
+0	-0
-0.7	+0
-0	-0.5
-0.7	-0.5
+2.0	+1.22
+0.5	+0

For two of the twelve consecutive days, my portfolio was more volatile (-0.89, +.97). This is 16.7 percent more volatile day changes, *but* 83.3 percent less volatile for the rest of the time. The range for

SPY is 1.84 - (-1.36) = 3.2. For my portfolio, the range is smaller: 1.17 + 0.97 = 2.14. This is only 66 percent the size of the SPY range. Also, from when I started, SPY is up 2.9 percent and I'm up 4.53 percent.

Are you seeing something interesting, if not paradoxical? I am trading like crazy, and my portfolio is less volatile. This also translated into improved performance and growth. Why? It's because I am using Compound Yield as an odds enhancer. It has nonlinear properties. It is a geometric/exponential factor I'm using to advantage. If it could be executed perfectly, growth in value would be exponential. By exponential, I mean that one becomes two; two becomes four; four becomes sixteen, etc. Linear means that to double the speed of my bicycle, I have to pedal twice as fast. Wouldn't you want a geometric enhancer on your side?

However, my positions are not always perfect. Dividends may get cut, share prices go down, some stocks have been lied about, analysts get deceived. By trading, I progressively augment my winners. By taking profits, I'm reducing risk of principal loss by buying into positions as they go down. My principal gets diluted with free-trade money. I'm mitigating the adverse effect of declining positions as I weed out my losers. However imperfect my real-world results are, I'm still going to beat my benchmark progressively. SPY is trying to duplicate the performance of the S&P 500 but falls short because management expenses are extracted periodically. It is an ETF. Mutual funds are even worse in administrative costs. Additionally, SPY can't rid itself of losers because it has to duplicate the S&P holdings. How many mutual funds can consistently keep up with and beat the S&P? Not too many.

Compounding is such a powerful force that I can make mistakes along the way and still win big. I don't have to predict market swings, pick perfect winners, panic when prices drop on my positions, fret about the next bad news, worry about getting onboard an upswing, or wonder what's going to be popular next. This system has the answers to all those problems. I don't have to lose sleep. I don't have to drive myself nuts. I'm confident that Compound Yield will have the answer for whatever question I can throw at it. Can you buy into this? Can you see and believe it? Can you trust and count on it? You bet, and this is a bet I'll take any day.

Because this strategy injures no one (there doesn't have to be a winner and a loser), it is not a zero-sum game. I believe it is God blessed. In the beauty of His infinite universe, it was already there. It just had to be discovered. Because it is something deducible by anyone, everyone has the God-given right to use it. It is a gift to you. It's God's gift to you. It has been there all the time until it was needed. I'm really just the conduit through which it has arrived. Given where our country is headed, I suggest we climb aboard and throttle up!

Maintaining Highway Speed

So far, we've accelerated the portfolio, and this has been relatively easy. It can be done rationally and quickly. We just needed to pick high-yield safe stocks that have strong fundamentals. By focusing on yield, we really did not have to figure out market timing, market direction, what stocks are popular, where the stock is in its trading cycle, or any of those traditional concerns. Optimizing yield accelerated the portfolio to roughly $77,000 annual income. I think that is extraordinarily surprising. Compared to SPY, which currently pays less than 2 percent, the results are impressive. This $77,000 now represents a 7.2 percent return annually over the whole portfolio. The rule of seventy-two tells us that we can expect to double this in ten years. I think we could tighten our belts and be comfortable in a conservative retirement. I like to think of this as having reached cruising speed of seventy-two mph!

How do we maintain it? What can the system tell us? It is remarkable to have a system to answer a question, but it is truly magical to have a system just waiting for someone to ask a question of it. By focusing on secure and rising dividends as well as yield, we'll find answers over and over again. These answers are several, and all are risk-managed. First, the process we started with continues to work. Our yield focus will need to change to adjusted yield, however. We'll get to this in a bit. Second, the original principal continues to be risk-managed. By taking profits, we reduce principal in any given position. Third, as we buy down into positions, we dilute the original principal with free-trade cash. Fourth, we don't game, chase, manipulate, predict, or guess at market direction. We greet whatever may come. We don't gamble. The system continues to tell us what to do. Fifth, we continue to size positions. We catch them up when low and sell off what has gone up. If we bought down into a position and the position then increases as the stock goes up, we sell off enough shares to bring it back down to $25,000 or 2.5 percent. Often, we have a net loss in the position by taking this trade, but it's less severe, and our yield is a little better on remaining shares. We did not lose any additional money because this loss was already priced into the total portfolio value.

Adjusted yield and dividend-loss cost become key factors in decision-making when we are dealing with a mature portfolio. Nearly all positions have been sized. Essentially, all passengers are onboard until the next trade day. Dividend-cost loss becomes visible when we look at what happens to our estimated annual portfolio yield following each trade. We sell enough shares to take profits off the table. Each share has a dividend yield associated with it. We must account for it and adjust our gross profit by it. Calculation of the loss is simple. We just multiply the profit by the share dividend yield divided by 100 (to convert percent to a decimal). This figure tells us how much return these shares would have made in income for a year if they were not sold to take profits. This then is subtracted off the gross expected profit to produce the adjusted profit. Next, we want to know what the dividend loss looks like compared to the adjusted profit—essentially, a negative yield value. This percent is the lowest return we can accept from our next trade. If a new position is opened and it has a lower yield, we'll see an overall decline in return for the portfolio. That's not to say we can't do it; it just reminds us to think the trade through prior to executing. It may be worth doing if you're convinced that the new position has upward momentum and you plan to make up the loss by taking profits. Now that's a true trader! I've chosen to do the comparison to the adjusted profit rather than the gross profit to give a little extra margin to exceed. Just another way we are risk-managing. By adhering to the rule, our portfolio yield always increases. A full example of this set-up can be seen in the "Growing with the Plan" section, e-mail dated 8/6/12.

Here, I'll use one position as an example:

Stock Symbol	Price	Cost of Position	Gross Profit	I'm Up	Present Stock Yield	Dividend Cost Loss	Adjusted Profit
XYZ	$22.50	$25,000	$1,500	3%	9%	$135.00	$1,365.00

Dividend cost loss: $1,500 x 9% divided by 100 = $135.00

Loss yield equals $135 divided by $1,365 X 100 = 9.9%

If we opened a new position, we'd have to be sure that the yield is at least 9.9%. Not easy to find. We probably want to pass on this trade.

I must digress here. My next thought came as an epiphany for me. Although I was very pleased to think that my returns have come so far that I now would have to find very high-yield positions, I also was alarmed that accomplishing this might not be so easy. One way to achieve it would be to just allow the market to climb further so that my percent profits would climb with it. The higher the profit/free cash, the lower the dividend yield I would need on a new or old position to replace the lost revenue (from shares sold to capture these profits). Again my anxiety rose, because that would mean I would have to gamble on the market direction prior to acting. This would be a tremendous flaw in the system. Fortunately, the system is built to answer whatever may be posed to it.

I've learned a lot about myself in the process of developing Compound Yield. I had to create something to help me control my own anxiety, and this formula does that at every turn, especially sharp ones. The investor and trader in me get satisfied simultaneously. The only leap of faith required is the belief that my positions are fundamentally sound enough to pay the promised dividend. Everything else transpires as a natural consequence of market direction. When share prices go up, progressive profit-taking serves as my trailing stop. Of anything, I'm most anxious when I've been short in the market. My answer for this now is to buy down into positions and wait for the short-covering rally to follow (which it will). I sell into it and take profits. I accomplish a higher yield on my remaining shares and take profits to boot! I love it! Should the market be flat, I'm earning a high yield on my holdings. All the while, I'm preparing for the next bear market run or bear market. Should the markets progressively decline, I've got plenty of income to buy things on the cheap. When the trend changes for an upswing, I not only ride up also, but I'm riding up on an exponential curve. I've been compounding all along. The results are amazing.

I manage my anxiety by exerting control. Because I can easily determine a dividend history and study fundamentals, I really enhance the likelihood of success. Once I've made my pick, the system takes care of the rest. I really can't see a market climate that this strategy can't succeed in. My confidence continues to grow with use. I see my portfolio's transformation as divinely influenced for my benefit. A pure mutual-fund 401K/retirement plan has none of these protections built in. Additionally, my retirement funds rarely kept up with their respective indices, let alone beat them. Even with rebalancing periodically, they fell short—way short. The amount of dividends produced for reinvestment was small anyway. The Compound Yield strategy prepares itself for the worst of times (long bear-market periods) by having the income necessary to sustain a retiree through no growth. For sideways-trading market periods, both income and capital gain will be available to sustain the retiree. In full bull markets, the retiree will gleefully take profits. If everything is up, the retiree doesn't have to worry about buying down into positions and taking profits to reinvest. He or she will be fine just taking off capital gains monthly. Personally, I've seen nothing as solid as this strategy for long—and very long-term results. My conviction cannot be any stronger. Well, that was some digression . . . but that was some epiphany! We'll now get back to the discussion.

Having a mature portfolio has its advantages. The Compound Yield strategy really can combine well with other strategies. As each position now is associated with a higher yield, we have to pay a little attention. Since most of our positions will be held for a long while, they stand to benefit from rising dividends each year. This could be up to an average of 6 percent or so. Let's assume 3 percent. We're on cruise control at 7.2 percent (72 mph). Any rising dividend actually reduces the 7.2 percent we have to have meet or exceed on average overall. If we came into a new year and each of our position's dividend went up by 3 percent, effectively, that 7.2 percent yield need is reduced to 4.2 percent for this new year. The effect would be magnified if we had bought down into the stock over the preceding year. More risk management built in, wouldn't you say? Finding stocks that pay a 4 percent or 5 percent dividend certainly is easier than finding a solid one to consistently pay a higher dividend.

Another way we can trade into a position with a lower yield would be to adjust for the dividend-loss cost. Let's say we had a trade day outcome of $16,000 net adjusted profit associated with a 9.5 percent negative dividend-cost yield. We're interested in stock ABC that is tremendously capable of paying an 8 percent dividend. The problem is 8 minus 9.5 equals a -1.5 percent yield difference. If we do this trade, the overall annual income on our portfolio would drop slightly. To avoid this, we can use our cash account, which should have a few thousand dollars in it to help us. We calculate how much we need to add to the $16,000 to still give us the income we need off the position:

$16,000 x 9.5 / 8 = $19,000

$16,000 associated with 9.5 percent dividend cost loss

+ $3,000 cash not associated with any loss

$16,000 x 0.095 = $1,520 annual income

$19,000 x 0.08 = $1,520.

Where do we get this cash? We should always generate and regenerate cash from trade day. We just save some. Plus, dividends are coming in monthly because this portfolio is already bringing in $77,000 a year.

Some of us who are gamblers can try to generate cash by pure trading plans. Again, it's your money. One safer way than outright trading might be to follow sectors and subsectors looking for the highest likelihood of buying a position that you progressively take profits on. Your own portfolio clues you in. Recall that for me, PFE, T, LLY, BP, and DDD continue to have profits taken off. I could add a telecommunication ETF or a pharmaceutical ETF. However, my overall portfolio would temporarily lose some dividend yield (because they generally pay a lower dividend). I would be doing it to progressively take off profits to buy a long-term position with the yield I wanted. It would be my gamble. By using low dividend yielding ETFs, we are gambling. We are essentially doing a swing trade, and we're taking an overnight risk. If I chose to use this strategy, I'd probably be following the position a few times a day and have a stop-loss in place. It can be a little tense, but there is nothing to preclude other strategies. It's still your choice.

Some Interesting Things

Some of my individual holdings have interesting properties that I found to be useful.

- JQC Nuveen CR Strategies Inc COM Shares: High income focus in secured and second-lien loans.
- MCN Madison Claymore Call and Equity FD COM: High income focus augmented by call options.
- EXG Eaton Vance Tax Managed GLB DV EQ COM: High income; uses calls also.
- ETY Eaton Vance Tax Managed Dividend Equity Income: Income first, growth second.

My broker really helped find these at a discount. I wouldn't have found these positions on my own in time.

- WEA Western Asset Premier Bond Fund: Has paid eleven cents/share monthly since 2010. As soon as I see it red, I think about buying more. Remember, a Compound Yield shark deals with loans for which neither the principal nor the interest rate is fixed. Here, I know one variable and can look to act quickly.
- UTG UTG Reaves Utility Incomes: Steady monthly rate of eleven cents/share and some special distributions.
- PSEC Prospect Capital Corporation: Steady ten cents monthly dividend.

Preferred Stocks:

- PYY PFD plus Goldman GSC4: 6 percent
- BCS.A BRCLY Sponsored ADR: 7.1 percent
- BAC.J Bank of America: 7.25 percent
- AEH AEGON NV PERP: 6.375 percent

My broker found these preferred stocks at a discount. When I first started to think more about income, these and the first group above formed the basis of generating income for reinvesting. This was my solution for not being able to contribute further to a rollover IRA. Now, the yield on my entire principal is 7.2 percent. At this point, I can start thinking about taking profits on my preferred stocks. I'll probably do this when I'm up 20 percent or more on any one of them.

- UIL UIL HLDG Corp. Utility income: Has paid forty-three cents/share quarterly since 2002. When share prices drop, I buy.
- TOT Total SA Sponsored ADR and AZN AstraZeneca ADR: Based in Europe and elsewhere; share prices suffered in the European meltdown. This brought up the dividend yield a lot. They are great companies, and I was able to start new positions with the yields I wanted.

The choices available are huge. I like to pick ones that produce consistently the yield I want. It is even better if the position is easy to follow and easy to remember by its uniqueness.

Driving This Home

This component of the discourse is really of importance to me. I'll describe the mindset that really helps me keep my eyes clearly on the ball. Compound Yield is a story of dark clouds (defensive) with silver linings (no losing trades). It is strongly defensive, and all risk is managed as a natural consequence of plan execution. I've tried to write this book like a blueprint of instruction. I'll try to drive home explicitly the mindset of compound yield. Fundamentally, I do not believe that stock prices reflect the value of anything—and even less so, the true value of any company. Owning a stock is not owning a part of a company. It's owning the expectation that you own a piece of the company. Ownership here is as imaginary as thinking you own your house when you're upside down in it. What is real is cash in your pocket or cash due to your account from dividends or distributions. Owning stock does give us the right, however, to be in the casino. At the blackjack table, I much prefer being the house than the drinking player.

The rule of seventy-two usually is used to make a best guess as to when the value of your portfolio will double. Alternatively, it can best-guess what rate of return will be needed to double your portfolio value in a specified time period. Here I'm using it to determine when my income stream will double independent of my portfolio value. Using it this way, I can benchmark my progress exactly. It tells me a specific monthly goal and, consequently, I can determine how much trading will be necessary to achieve this goal. As I stated earlier, my original principal is now earning 7.2 percent annually. If I maintain this rate, I'll double my income in ten years. Over the first year, $77,000 x 7.2/100 = $5,544. This divided by twelve equals $462 monthly. For the following year, this would become $462 + ($462 x 7.2/100) = $495/month. Over the course of the next year, no losing trades will actually help exponentially. Whether stock prices for an individual holding climb or not, the total number of portfolio shares keeps increasing. This is the growth I'm concerned with. Each share is contributing to income. I'm looking more for a small climb in share price over a lot more shares to trade with than a larger rise in price over fewer shares. By buying down into positions, we aggressively increase income per share. When an increase in a dividend is declared, the benefit to us has been purposefully magnified by cost averaging. None of these events results in a linear increase; each one is designed for geometric change. Compounding is nonlinear. We're capturing a blessed secret from the universe and applying it for our benefit consistently over and over. We pay exact attention and achieve this with every trade day by being sure we account for the annual dividend loss on the shares sold for profit. If we take this loss and divide it by the gross profit, this gives us the break-even point for yield on any new position. By dividing instead by the adjusted profit, we've built in a safety factor. When we meet or exceed this, we know that we are moving the portfolio income ahead consistently.

This shows up on my account Web page. My account's homepage has a specific click-on page that shows my projected income monthly and annually. It even breaks down which stocks are paying dividends and how much for the next twelve months. Seeing this grow is a rush for me. This drives me to never leave profits on the table. Emotionally, I'm no longer content seeing my positions green. I see these as food left on the table for my dogs to get, and they've already been fed! Alternatively, I feel compassion for my red positions. I know that they are producing maximum income. This makes me want to alleviate their stress by increasing their numbers. I buy down. The focus on yield is everything. Any action that compounds yield produces a geometric change over time. Knowing this drives me harder to beat my monthly benchmark. Instead of retiring in ten years, I want to pull this closer to today, and I want this pull to be gravitational—an exponential effect. I want retirement accelerating at me. The whole process makes mathematical sense. The process is morally correct because it harms no one. It is not a zero-sum game. Someone doesn't lose to the extent of someone else winning. Because it is simply following a law derived from the universe, it shares in the intrinsic perfection of the universe. I share in this perfection by sharing it with you. The yield I harvest will be nonlinear. It will be exponential.

Dividend return is the best of all free trading because it is free and clear of any encumbrance. There is no annual dividend loss to account for like we have to on shares sold to capture profits. Building dividend income is crucial. From 6/29/12 through 8/21/12, I had thirteen trade days with free-trade profits adding up to over $300,000. Isn't that incredible to think that over that short period, there was that much profit just waiting to be used to buy income? On my original principal, that is almost 30 percent. Taking this profit and just reinvesting at 5 percent would increase my annual return by $15,000. As you may recall, I mentioned that in retirement, we should really tap only 4 percent of our retirement funds as an annual income. On a million-dollar portfolio, this is $40,000. In just shy of two months, I could have increased my income by $15,000. This $55,000 is an annual income increase of 37.5 percent! Pardon me for a moment while I feel around for my eyes on the floor, as they have popped out of my head. I'm pretty sure I'm on to something here—something big.

At present, I'm up in total return 5.1 percent from when I started with Scott and Stringfellow. SPY is up about 4 percent. I'm still up 1.1 percent over SPY, even though SPY really has been on a run. I haven't climbed as fast, but I've also been less volatile. My income continues to increase progressively. You're probably wondering, "Gee, I would have thought he'd be a little further ahead." Certainly a reasonable thought. Recall, however, that exponential growth starts slowly, and when it is clear that something is happening, the results become explosive. Let's look at a few more things.

Compound Yield as a strategy really becomes an excellent preparation for the next downturn or bear market. While still taking excellent advantage of an up market, it's preparing for the downturn. Let's assume that the market positions tank 20 percent, predominately on the basis of emotion. If dividends keep being paid, what happens? Say stock XYZ drops from $10.00/share to $8.00/share—a 20 percent decline. It continues to pay a 5 percent annual dividend. That's $0.5 divided by $8.00 x 100 = 6.25 percent. When we buy down on the new shares purchased, the new dividend yield is 6.25 percent, not 5 percent. This 6.25 percent minus 5 percent equals 1.25 percent, and 1.25 divided by 5 multiplied 100 equals 25 percent. Did you notice that the stock dropped 20 percent and our yield went up on new shares by 25 percent? That 5 percent more is just extra evidence that our odds-enhancer is nonlinear. When we pay attention, all of our actions help increase yield predictably. We just need to be a little compulsive and a little patient.

During a bear market, trading for profit-taking may be considerably more difficult. Our dividend income is what we have to optimize our yield with. It will be easy to buy into any of our positions and be confident that we are increasing our portfolio income when all of our positions have dropped. We need to worry less about outpacing the market in good times and focus on increasing yield on our portfolio. Growth certainly will follow as the total number of shares in the portfolio increases rapidly by free-trading profits along the way. Our best protection going into a bear market is to enter it having built the highest revenue stream in good times. The better we go in, the better we do in the following bull market. If we went into a bull market with twice the revenue stream as a consequence of adding a huge number of shares, we're going to do more than twice as well riding the bull. This is where we'll really see the benefit of Compound Yield. We'll be riding up on the exponential curve. We just need a little patience.

Again, this strategy does not preclude others. In a bear market, not everything may be going down. Traders normally look at sectors, subsectors, other assets, currencies, metals, etc. ETFs can be used to take advantage of these while taking profits along the way to reinvest in our best down positions. Be proactive. There are plenty of ways to protect and optimize income.

Finally, you have to do this for yourself. Your broker can't do this for just one client. If he could, he really would be entitled to a large commission, and rightfully so. Plain mutual funds can't do it either. On Monday, March 9, 2010, SPY was at a low of $68.11. On August 24, 2012, SPY was at $141.51. Calculate $141.51 minus $68.11, divide by $68.11, and multiply 100 for 107.8% total return over about three and a half years. Do you recall saying to yourself, "Hey, my retirement funds just doubled?" I certainly didn't. I'm actually a little angry about that fact. Look at the one-year, three-year, five-year, and ten-year total returns for your retirement funds, including sales charges. Do you see any generating 30 percent annually for the last three years? My point is that traditional 401K retirement plans are hopelessly doomed to fail. They are being traded against. Mutual-fund performances have paled terribly by comparison. I had no problem selling my losers. You shouldn't either. Investing is still possible, just not by long-term buy and hold. My eyes were opened when I got an education from a professional trading academy. Education has always been my best advantage. I'm done kicking myself for not having done it sooner. Better investing necessitates being a better trader. You can have the mindset of both a trader and an investor; they don't have to be seen as mutually exclusive.

Now I want you to clearly see what I see and the way I see it. If compound interest produces an exponential curve that will eventually allow me to retire, I want to move that curve to the left. By pulling the curve to the left one trade day at a time, I'll get to retire sooner. Compound Yield, as I've adapted it here, is compounding compound interest. In my earlier example, 7.2% dividend return will allow me to double my income in ten years (using the rule of 72). If on any position, I can capture one year's worth of dividend in a single trade and I reinvest at 7.2% (having accounted for the dividend cost loss), I've knocked off one year to doubling the income on that position. In other words, ten years now becomes nine years. If I can pull this off on every position, I retire in nine years. I want to do this again and again. Not only do I want to be on an exponential income curve, I don't want to wait 10 years to arrive with the income stream I need. I want to pull to curve closer to me. I want to shift it to the left. I want to repeat the process often enough such that retirement accelerates toward me. I think of compound interest as magical. I believe Compound Yield to be MIRACULOUS. This is the quintessential function that separates this strategy from any investing or trading plan I have ever seen.

Odds, Ends, and Disclaimers

I sleep best at night when I'm confident that I've been of service. Although I share the usual disclaimer that "past performance does not guarantee future success," I believe in the true value of the Compound Yield formula. It will continue to be a major part of my portfolio management. There are probably as many trading and investment plans out there as there are people to use them. I sincerely hope these pages will help you design for yourself your own trading and investment plan. We have to be responsible for these ourselves. Having a solid plan and sticking to it is crucial for your long-term success. In fact, my trading instructors emphasized repeatedly that failure almost always results from deviating from the plan. Deviation usually destroys risk protection and consequently increases the likelihood of being slaughtered. The traditional 401K retirement plans really have no risk protection, and they can't win consistently in a trader's market. Arm yourself with this fact and act on your own behalf. Get training professionally. Online Trading

Academy did this for me. I hope there is one in your city. Be joyful if this will cause you to act. That was my intention.

I've often wondered what my place will be in the investing and trading world. I think that writing this book has helped me with that. If I had to define myself—or, for that matter, the Compound Yield investor—I'd have to say that I've become a sort of market shark as well, a specialized one who deals in high-interest loans where neither the principal nor the interest is fixed. I'm a loan shark! Compound Yield sharks are good and virtuous ones by virtue of their actions. They exist really for the common good. They victimize no one. Their focus is great and precisely on yield. Action is predictable and without emotion, adhering to precise rules predicated upon protecting and increasing yield. They are benevolent and kind. They satisfy speculating sharks and short-covering panicked sharks by selling them what they seek—shares—*but* for a profit. Their presence helps to blunt stock-market volatility. The wind is taken out of unrestrained market assent. They are disciplinarians, countering attempts to short the market. Compound Yield sharks are champions of the true investor. World-class fighters, they never lose a trade. They are the top of the ecosystem they help protect. Readily recognizable by the color of their skin (green—US minted currency green), they yield to no one and only to *yield*. I hope these pages will select for and breed Compound Yield sharks!

The Catalyst

As a physician and a neurologist, in particular, I'm in part a scientist. Importantly, neither science nor scientists created the universe. Instead, science discovers its truths, and these can often be described by equations. Scientists then use these equations to create things. This is precisely true of my Compound Yield strategy. Try to get your mind around it. This strategy is a mathematical derivation to produce increasing income—that is, yield. The math is, thankfully, fairly straightforward and modestly simple. Activation of the strategy provides clear answers that are mathematically driven. The strategy is able to answer all of our questions emotionlessly on this basis. That is the beauty not to be missed here. The strategy hinges upon the intrinsic properties of stocks . . . their nature, so to speak. It fuses the best of investing (rational) with the best of trading (emotional). The outcome is consistency, and this shows up as increasing income. The yield on our principal is sustained or increases over time. We don't take trades that can't accomplish this. Again, the decision is mathematical and calculated. The answers to whatever we face are already built into the system. We just have to discover them! All we have to do is decide which stocks we want and at what yield. This is where we have to double-check ourselves to be sure our choices are rational and sound. After all, as humans, it's part of our nature to gamble and take risks. There is no gambling, no gaming, no manipulation, and no victim in the Compound Yield formula. Activation of the system produces a rational predictable response/outcome. All we have to do is put rational information into it.

What is required of us is to choose the highest-quality stocks/instruments our resources tell us about, at a yield we would like to start with. The system is built for volatility especially. It manages the emotions of fear and greed for us. We just have to detach from our emotions.

Honest to God, what I've shown you here will become my new life's work to spread. I hope you can get your arms around it. If you are an engineer, scientist, math and science teacher, or any other professional who is analytical, you *need* this system. Analytical people tend to be lousy traders. They can't make trading decisions fast enough. This is especially true for day-trading equities, trading futures, and trading currency/FOREX. What happens is that you'll either be stopped out of a trade or you'll not let your winners run long enough. My trading instructors told me that with good stop-losses in place, a trader can be profitable if he or she can let one winner "run" long enough out of four trades. I have too much of a trigger finger, and I too am a lousy trader.

The Compound Yield strategy is my answer to trading. I always get to win, and I trade a lot. I like to invest where my money counts. I like income and especially growing income. I like to calculate rather than take impulsive chances. I like a little time to act.

The strategy has growth as a secondary consequence. Despite all the trading for income I've done, I'm still up in portfolio value against my benchmark. How? Because we are constantly selling high and buying low or at market, I'm still outpacing SPY. I'm accumulating more shares rather than waiting for capital appreciation on a position. Each of these is making income for me to do it over and over.

I hope this book will be a catalyst for a revolution. We need many, many more Compound Yield sharks. In fact, the more the better, and I hope millions will quickly join me. Volatility should smooth over time, and the trillions of dollars sidelined will start to come back into the market. When they do, they will be conservative and looking for income. The shelves of my store will be full of items for sale, but not at fire-sale prices. What could be better for me, for you, and for every other go-getter out there presently unprotected by a defined-benefit pension plan? I truly believe that redemption has been granted to me by God, and the only requirement imposed on me is to share it.

Calculation Template

Ticker Symbol	Yield	Share Cost	Cost of Position	Amount Up	% Up	Sell Shares	Annual Dividend Loss	Adjusted Profit

Definitions

Ticker Symbol: Be sure to record this right. Mistakes are costly.

Yield: The present yield—or, better yet, your specific yield. This is calculated by the total number of shares you own divided into your total position cost. This gives you the average cost of your shares. Look up the present dividend and multiply to get the annual dividend. Next, divide the annual dividend by your average share price and multiply by 100 to get your specific yield.

Share Cost: I just use the closing cost from the day before. I usually set up the night before Trade Day.

Cost of Position: Dollar amount.

Amount Up: How far the position is in the green.

% Up: The green amount divided by the position cost.

Sell Shares: The number of shares to be sold to capture profits. Divide up the amount by the present cost of a share.

Annual Dividend Loss: The up position amount multiplied by the yield and then divided by 100.

Adjusted Profit: The up amount minus the annual dividend loss amount.

Process

We sum up the up amounts to get the gross profit; we sum up the annual dividend loss; we sum up adjusted profit. Next, we calculate what yield we have to meet or exceed to keep the portfolio income increasing. If we simply divided the dividend-cost loss total by the gross profit total and multiplied by 100, we would find the break-even yield. I've chosen instead to do the calculation on adjusted profit to give us a harder margin. By doing it this way, we are assured that either buying down into old positions or buying a new position will push the portfolio yield ahead consistently.

Resources

I really have settled on just a few. They are easy to use and have been reliable.

What really got me moving is when I reviewed my first monthly briefing from Carla Pasternak's High-Yield Investing from Street Authority (www.streetauthority.com). It is a paid-for service, but the cost has been well worth it.

By following sectors and subsectors as well as my portfolio itself, I'm clued in to areas to look for a new position or a complementary one. This is particularly true for very hot sectors in which the best trade for me is to run with momentum taking profits as I go, and then buy down into the position to increase yield. I use Sector Timing Report (www.sectortimingreport.com). This is also a monthly briefing paid-for service.

FINVIZ.com is a free site where I can use the stock selector to prospect new positions.

OptionArmy.com is important for me to look at to find out what the overnight futures market has done. I like to set up every detail of my trades on Sunday for Monday. Before I execute, I like to be sure nothing crazy has been brewing overnight when the US markets were closed to trading. I also check what's been up with the foreign markets. The whole world is connected. If something is amiss in the foreign exchanges, you can bet it shows up after market opening here.

Seeking Alpha (seekingalpha.com) offers absolutely great articles and searches. It's free. You can also just use Google or Bing.

MSN Money (money.msn.com) also has great articles, and I like to its StockScouter rater to check out the opinion for present positions and ones I'm looking into.

I have an IRA on E*TRADE (us.etrade.com), and I love looking at snapshots, charts, analysts' ratings, insider trading, and fundamentals for my stock picks. This is where I can easily back-test any stock and see how the strategy would likely have done.

Robert Naguszewski (Nag-goo-chef-ski) MD is a board-certified internist, and is also board-certified by the American Board of Neurology and Psychiatry. He has had broad experience with pain management as well as rehabilitation. Out of his own need to fix his retirement future, he created the Compound Yield formula. Drawing on many years of clinical experience dealing with all varieties of human emotion and fusing this knowledge with his desire to make scientific and mathematical sense out of the marketplace, he put together a predictable model for action. One of his basic assumptions is that trading is emotion being dissipated. Investing in an emotional market becomes senseless unless a structure can be put in place to consistently increase return through income. Stocks have intrinsic properties independent from market emotion that can be harnessed mathematically and scientifically to create this structure. Unifying emotion and science in a manner aligned with spiritual laws governing respect and morality should be able to unlock the universe to the benefit of all. Seeing his plan manifest the desired result over time prompted him to write this book. His need to share it with you is motivated by this understanding.

Made in United States
North Haven, CT
16 November 2023

44111358R00067